THE
SAINTS'
LITTLE BOOK OF
WISDOM

The Essential Teachings

Compiled by Andrea Kirk Assaf

HarperCollins*Publishers*
1 London Bridge Street
London SE1 9GF
www.harpercollins.co.uk

First published by HarperCollins*Publishers* in 2016

1 3 5 7 9 10 8 6 4 2

Copyright © 2016 HarperCollins*Publishers*
Compiled by Andrea Kirk Assaf and Kelly Anne Leahy
Cover design by e-Digital Design
Cover image credit: Cover image: Fresco, Rila Monastery, Bulgaria by
Asaf Eliason/Shutterstock
Text design by e-Digital Design

A catalogue record for this book is available from the British Library

ISBN 978-0-00-795456-8

Printed in the United Kingdom

MIX

Paper from responsible sources

FSC™ C007454

FSC™ is a non-profit international organisation established to promote the responsible
management of the world's forests. Products carrying the FSC label are independently certified
to assure consumers that they come from forests that are managed to meet the social, economic
and ecological needs of present and future generations, and other controlled sources.

Find out more about HarperCollins and the environment at

www.harpercollins.co.uk/green

THE
SAINTS'
LITTLE BOOK OF
WISDOM

The Essential Teachings

Compiled by Andrea Kirk Assaf

WILLIAM
COLLINS

Dost thou hold wisdom to be anything other than truth, wherein we behold and embrace the supreme good?

St. Augustine

The lives of the saints are a model for the lives of the rest of men.

St. Ambrose

Contents

A Note to the Reader

"A saint is a sinner who just keeps trying."

This adage, attributed to various sources, might just summarize this whole compilation of quotes. The rather intimidating implied message is that these individuals whom we revere as wise and holy were, in their lifetimes, frail human beings just like us—possessing the whole variety of temptations, temperaments, and responsibilities as you and I today. They were the ones who persevered, who didn't give in to despair or despondency.

There is a striking commonality in the wisdom of the saints that speaks to us across the ages, cultures, and classes, and that led these men and women to sanctity. The desire to know, love, serve, and unite with God guided their consciences and actions. Their shared goal was the pursuit of wisdom and holiness through the practice of the virtues, not just for the sake of self-perfection but, on the contrary, in order to empty the self to be filled with the Holy Spirit.

If this goal seems too lofty, if the path of virtue too arduous, take these saints along with you as expert guides. Tuck this small volume in your pocket, or in a friend's bag, to go along for the daily commute, the tedious wait in line, the short lunch break. Read one quote a day and jot down your reflections or your prayer intentions for that saint's intercession in the white space below the quote or in the journal pages. The embellished journal pages at the back of the book could be used as a place to collect your own favorite saints' quotes that don't appear in this compilation. If you are gifting this book to someone, you might use the journal pages to include a personal note or quotes by the recipient's patron saints. You can customize this little pocket book to make it your own personal journal of conversations with the community of saints who accompany us on our journey through life.

May the wisdom of the saints inspire us sinners to just keep trying.

Andrea Kirk Assaf
Easter 2016
Rome, Italy

Reflections by
the Compilers

When I was a little girl about the age of seven, I would carry around with me a pocket-sized children's book of the lives of the saints. The glamorous, technicolor illustrations of St. Helena the Empress, St. Joan of Arc, and St. Elizabeth, Queen of Hungary, are still fresh in my mind's eye. I became so enraptured with their dramatic, fairy tale-like biographies that my older sisters teasingly nicknamed me 'Sister Andrea.' Fast-forward several decades—a husband and three children later—and I am still enthralled by the lives of the saints and have passed that fascination on to the next generation. In our home-school curriculum, we read and discuss the story of the saint of the day in the sanctoral cycle of the Catholic Church. It may well be the only part of the curriculum the kids actually ask for without prodding.

Over time, these saints have become part of our family culture. We choose individual special saints each New Year, choose patron saints for our family, our home-school, and our undertakings. We invoke the protection of Santa Francesca Romana, patron saint of auto travel, each time we set out in our family van. We take pilgrimages to their shrines, revere their relics, walk where they once walked, and draw analogies between their lives and our own.

Often this communication with the community of saints is intentional, but sometimes they enter our lives by surprise. The other morning we happened upon someone new in our daily readings: St. Benedict Joseph Labré, a perpetual pilgrim who would sleep in the Colosseum during his Rome wanderings. Upon his canonization, he became the patron saint of the homeless and is now buried in a church near the historic center of the Eternal City of Rome. My ten-year-old daughter, inspired by his story, brought the computer to the table and found (thanks to Wikipedia and Google Maps!) the location of his eternal resting place in the church of Santa Maria ai Monti. A field-trip plan was hatched!

This little book will also become part of our family's conversations and adventures with the saints as a supplement to the biographies we read. The short quotes of wisdom and advice can serve not only as sources for personal reflection, but also for family discussion of the various themes these quotes address, such as virtue and suffering. God only knows where

the saints will lead us next, but of this we can
be sure: their road is narrow and arduous but
their way is both tried and true.

Andrea Kirk Assaf

It is impossible to walk through the streets of Kolkata, India, and not feel the presence of the small figure who hurriedly moved among the 'poorest of the poor,' going about God's business. Nearly 20 years after her death, Mother Teresa's love is palpable even in the city's darkest corners. For this reason, I was motivated to pick up *Come be My Light*, a compilation of Mother Teresa's letters to her spiritual director. Instead of an account of saintly joy and inner peace, I read the story of a woman who suffered almost relentlessly with loneliness and despair towards the end of her life. My childhood perceptions of a saint's earthly journey were upended, and I then understood that the road to sanctity is not a straight path to spiritual perfection, but rather the humble willingness to persevere in overcoming our temptations and failures.

As I helped to compile this collection of quotes, I was confirmed in the belief that sainthood is not only attainable, but that we were created for it. When we fail, our saintly predecessors are there to help guide and encourage us along the way. As the saints attest in these chapters, when we recognize and embrace this path with sincerity, we open the doors to a new world for ourselves, one especially prepared for us by God, full of immeasurable peace and joy.

Kelly Anne Leahy

PART ONE

Virtue:

the Path to Sanctity

To reform. Every day a little. This has to be your constant task if you really want to become a saint.

St. Josemaría Escriva

Men who strive after a virtuous and God-loving life are zealous for virtues of the soul, as a possession which is inalienably their own and brings eternal comfort. They use temporal things only as much as is necessary and as God wishes and provides, using them with gladness and all gratitude, even if they be very moderate. For a rich table feeds bodies, as being material, whereas knowledge of God, self-mastery, goodness, doing good to others, piety, and meekness deify the soul.

St. Anthony of Egypt

Holiness does not consist in one exercise or another, but is a disposition of the heart, which renders us humble and little in the hands of God, conscious of our weakness, and confident, even daringly confident, in His fatherly goodness.

St. Thérèse of Lisieux

D o not try to excuse your faults; try to correct them.

St. John Bosco

Restraint, meekness, chastity, steadfastness, patience, and similar great virtues are given us by God as weapons to resist and oppose the tribulations we meet with, and to help us when they occur. So if we train ourselves in the use of these powers and keep them always ready, then nothing that may befall us will ever be hard, grievous, destructive, or unbearable, for all would be overcome by the virtues we possess. Those whose soul is not intelligent never think of this, for they do not believe that all happens for our good, in order that our virtues should shine forth and that we should be crowned by God for them.

St. Anthony of Egypt

As to be holy is nothing else than to will what God wills, so to be wise is nothing else than to judge of things as God judges of them.

St. Vincent de Paul

A man who governs his passions is master of the world. We must either rule them, or be ruled by them. It is better to be the hammer than the anvil.

St. Dominic

Do not lose courage in considering your own imperfections, but instantly set about remedying them.

St. Francis de Sales

Sanctity consists in struggling, in knowing that we have defects and in heroically trying to overcome them. Sanctity, I insist, consists in overcoming those defects although we will still have defects when we die; for if not, as I have told you, we would become proud.

St. Josemaría Escrivá

Above all ... sanctity does not consist in being faithful for a day or a year but in persevering until death, we must use God as a shield which covers us completely because we are attacked from all sides.

St. Claude de la Colombière

For without a pure mind and a modeling of the life after the saints, a man could not possibly comprehend the words of the saints.

St. Athanasius

A man who does not know how to discriminate between good and evil has no right to judge who is good and who evil among men. A man who knows God, is good; when a man is not good, it means that he does not know (God) and will never be known (by Him): for the only means to know God is goodness.

St. Anthony of Egypt

The virtue of patience is the one which most assures us of perfection.

St. Francis de Sales

Sanctify yourself and you will sanctify
society.

St. Francis of Assisi

Conquer yourself each day from the very first moment, getting up on the dot, at a set time, without granting a single minute to laziness. If, with the help of God, you conquer yourself in that moment, you'll have accomplished a great deal for the rest of the day. It's so discouraging to find yourself beaten in the first skirmish!

St. Josemaría Escrivá

Let us remember that the heart of Jesus has called us not only for our own sanctification, but also for that of other souls. He wants to be helped in the salvation of souls.

St. Pio of Pietrelcina

The real conflict is the inner conflict. Beyond armies of occupation and the hecatombs of extermination camps, there are two irreconcilable enemies in the depth of every soul: good and evil, sin and love. And what use are the victories on the battlefield if we ourselves are defeated in our innermost personal selves.

St. Maximilian Kolbe

Only for today, I will devote ten minutes of my time to some good reading, remembering that just as food is necessary to the life of the body, so good reading is necessary to the life of the soul.

St. John XXIII

To be pleased at correction and reproofs shows that one loves the virtues which are contrary to those faults for which he is corrected and reproved. And, therefore, it is a great sign of advancement in perfection.

St. Francis de Sales

People who have no natural inclination to good must not be discouraged and give way to despair. They must not cease striving after a virtuous life pleasing to God, however inaccessible and unattainable it is to them. They too must take thought and have a care for themselves as best they can. For, although they may not reach the summit of virtue and perfection, by taking thought and caring for themselves in every possible way they will either become better or, at least, not worse—and this is no small profit to the soul.

St. Anthony of Egypt

If we wish to make any progress in the service of God we must begin every day of our life with new eagerness. We must keep ourselves in the presence of God as much as possible and have no other view or end in all our actions but the divine other.

St. Charles Borromeo

The means of salvation and sanctification are known to all; they are laid down in the Gospel, explained by the masters of the spiritual life, practiced by the saints, and necessary to all who wish to be saved and to attain perfection. They are humility of heart, continual prayer, mortification in all things, abandonment to Divine Providence and conformity to the will of God.

St. Louis de Montfort

Do not be afraid to be holy! Have the courage and humility to present yourselves to the world determined to be holy, since full, true freedom is born from holiness.

St. John Paul II

Persevere in your virtuous habits. Make it a practice ever and constantly to increase in the performance of good works.

St. Bonaventure

Holiness does not consist in doing extraordinary things. It consists in accepting, with a smile, what Jesus sends us. It consists in accepting and following the will of God.

St. Teresa of Calcutta

I have been all things unholy. If God can work through me, He can work through anyone.

St. Francis of Assisi

Think well. Speak well. Do well. These three things, through the mercy of God, will make a man go to Heaven.

St. Camillus de Lellis

That a soul is truly intelligent and virtuous is shown in a man's look, walk, voice, smile, conversation, and manner. In such a soul all has been transformed and has taken on its fairest aspect. Its God-loving mind, like a watchful doorkeeper, bars the entrance to evil and shameful thoughts.

St. Anthony of Egypt

To live is to change, and to be perfect is to have changed often.

Bl. John Henry Newman

God's invitation to become saints is for all, not just a few. Sanctity therefore must be accessible to all. In what does it consist? In a lot of activity? No. In doing extraordinary things? No, this could not be for everybody and at all times. Therefore, sanctity consists in doing good, and in doing this good in whatever condition and place God has placed us. Nothing more, nothing outside of this.

Bl. Louis Tezza

I would never want any prayer that would not make the virtues grow within me.

St. Teresa of Avila

PART TWO

Humility:
the Grandeur of the Small

Neither fear of God, nor mercy, nor faith, nor self-mastery, nor any other virtue can be achieved without humility. Moreover, humility destroys all the arrows of the enemy. All the saints followed the way of humility and labored at it ... Do you see the power of this virtue? Indeed there is nothing stronger than humility, for nothing can conquer it. If some affliction befalls a humble man, he immediately blames himself for deserving it and will not reproach or blame another. Thus he endures everything that may befall (him) untroubled, without grief, with perfect calm; and so he is angered by no one and angers none.

St. Dorotheos of Gaza

[G od] didn't attach salvation to knowledge or intelligence or wealth, nor to long experience or rare gifts that are not given to all. He attached it to something within the reach of everyone, absolutely everyone. Jesus attaches salvation to humility, to the act of making yourself little. That is all it takes to win Heaven.

Bl. Charles de Foucauld

Dear friend, show your gratitude to our Lord by becoming humble and obedient. Let us ask the Most Holy Virgin and the Holy Child Jesus for these two virtues for each other every day.

St. Bernadette

Ah, how true it is that we love ourselves too much and proceed with too much human prudence, that we may not lose an atom of our consideration! Oh, what a great mistake that is! The saints did not act thus.

St. Teresa of Avila

He Who is the beginning and the end, the ruler of the angels, made Himself obedient to human creatures. The creator of the heavens obeys a carpenter; the God of eternal glory listens to a poor virgin. Has anyone ever witnessed anything comparable to this? Let the philosopher no longer disdain from listening to the common laborer; the wise, to the simple; the educated, to the illiterate; a child of a prince, to a peasant.

St. Anthony of Padua

If so great and good a Lord, then, chose to appear despised, needy, and poor in this world, so that people who were in utter poverty and want and in absolute need of heavenly nourishment might become rich in Him by possessing the Kingdom of Heaven, then rejoice and be glad!

St. Clare of Assisi

Never say, 'what great things the saints do,' but, 'what great things God does in His saints.'

St. Philip Neri

Learn to be silent sometimes for the edification of others, that you may learn how to speak sometimes.

St. Vincent Ferrer

As gifts increase in you, let your humility grow, for you must consider that everything is given to you on loan.

St. Pio of Pietrelcina

Preach by example, and practice before the eyes of the young, what you wish them to accept.

St. John Baptiste de la Salle

Our Lord needs from us neither great deeds nor profound thoughts. Neither intelligence nor talents. He cherishes simplicity.

St. Thérèse of Lisieux

If we are, in fact, now occupied in good deeds, we should not attribute the strength with which we are doing them to ourselves. We must not count on ourselves, because even if we know what kind of person we are today, we do not know what we will be tomorrow.

St. Gregory the Great

The most powerful weapon to conquer the devil is humility. For, as he does not know at all how to employ it, neither does he know how to defend himself from it.

St. Vincent de Paul

There is more value in a little study of humility and in a single act of it than in all the knowledge in the world.

St. Teresa of Avila

The saints are like the stars. In His providence Christ conceals them in a hidden place that they may not shine before others when they might wish to do so. Yet they are always ready to exchange the quiet of contemplation for the works of mercy as soon as they perceive in their heart the invitation of Christ.

St. Anthony of Padua

He who wishes to be perfectly obeyed,
should give but few orders.

St. Philip Neri

We are taught to have humbleness of heart … by the statement in the Gospel: 'Learn of me, for I am meek and lowly in heart, and you shall find rest for your souls' (Matt 11.29). But this humbleness of heart is the same thing as is elsewhere called poverty in spirit, so that we are not to be lifted up in pride or seek after glory by a pretend humility, but rather that we abase ourselves with our whole heart.

St. Jerome

Paint the house of your soul with modesty
and lowliness and make it splendid with
the light of justice. Adorn it with the beaten
gold of good works, for walls and stones
embellish assiduously with faith
and generosity.

St. John Chrysostom

For it is clear that a man inclines himself
towards humility if, knowing that he can
achieve no virtue without God's help, he never
ceases to pray, asking God to show him mercy.
Thus a man who prays without ceasing, if he
achieves something, knows why he achieved
it, and can take no pride in it; for he cannot
attribute it to his own powers, but attributes

all his achievements to God, always renders
thanks to Him and constantly calls upon Him,
trembling lest he be deprived of help. Thus
he prays with humility and is made humble
by prayer. The more he progresses in virtue
the greater becomes his humility, and as his
humility grows he receives help and again
progresses in humility.

St. Dorotheos of Gaza

Humility is the only virtue that no devil can imitate. If pride made demons out of angels, there is no doubt that humility could make angels out of demons.

St. John Climacus

He who really wished to become a saint must never defend himself, except in a few rare cases, but always acknowledge himself in fault, even when what is alleged against him is untrue.

St. Philip Neri

If I were asked the secret of happiness, I should say self-forgetfulness and continual self-denial, which effectually destroy pride. The love of God should be strong enough to destroy all love for self.

Bl. Elizabeth of the Trinity

Let your old age be childlike, and your childhood like old age; that is, so that neither may your wisdom be with pride, nor your humility without wisdom.

St. Augustine

PART THREE

Love:
Living out Charity

Charity is the form, mover, mother, and root of all the virtues.

St. Thomas Aquinas

Each of you knows that the foundation of our faith is charity. Without it, our religion would crumble. We will never be truly Catholic unless we conform our entire lives to the two commandments that are the essence of the Catholic faith: to love the Lord, our God, with all our strength, and to love our neighbor as ourselves.

Bl. Pier Giorgio Frassati

We become what we love and who we love shapes what we become. If we love things, we become a thing. If we love nothing, we become nothing. Imitation is not a literal mimicking of Christ, rather it means becoming the image of the beloved, an image disclosed through transformation. This means we are to become vessels of God's compassionate love for others.

St. Claire of Assisi

Charity is a virtue of such power that it can both close the gates of hell and open wide the portals of eternal bliss. Charity provides the hope of salvation and alone renders us lovable in God's sight.

St. Bonaventure

Perfection of life is the perfection of love.
For love is the life of the soul.

St. Francis de Sales

There is no place for selfishness—and no place for fear! Do not be afraid, then, when love makes demands. Do not be afraid when love requires sacrifice.

St. John Paul II

It is not enough for us to say: 'I love God,' but I also have to love my neighbor. St. John says that you are a liar if you say you love God and you don't love your neighbor. How can you love God whom you do not see, if you do not love your neighbor whom you see, whom you touch, with whom you live? And so it is very important for us to realize that love, to be true, has to hurt. I must be willing to give whatever it takes not to harm other people and, in fact, to do good to them. This requires that I be willing to give until it hurts. Otherwise, there is not true love in me and I bring injustice, not peace, to those around me.

St. Teresa of Calcutta

Love suffers long and is kind; love does not envy; love does not parade itself, is not puffed up; does not behave rudely, does not seek its own, is not provoked, thinks no evil; does not rejoice in iniquity, but rejoices in the truth; bears all things, believes all things, hopes all things, endures all things.

St. Paul the Apostle

You know well enough that Our Lord does not look so much at the greatness of our actions, nor even at their difficulty, but at the love with which we do them.

St. Thérèse of Lisieux

An action of small value performed with much love of God is far more excellent than one of a higher virtue, done with less love of God.

St. Francis de Sales

The proof of love is in the works. Where love exists, it works great things. But when it ceases to act, it ceases to exist.

St. Gregory the Great

There is nothing which edifies others so much as charity and kindness, by which, as by the oil in our lamp, the flame of good example is kept alive.

St. Francis de Sales

You don't need to change to believe in my love, for it will be my belief in your love that will change you.

St. Teresa of Calcutta

Charity is the sweet and holy bond which links the soul with its Creator: it binds God with man and man with God.

St. Catherine of Siena

Since our Lord dwells in our soul, His prayer is ours, and I desire to partake of it unceasingly, keeping like a little pitcher beside the fountain, so that I may be able to give life to others by letting His inexhaustible streams of charity overflow on them. 'For them do I sanctify Myself, that they may be sanctified in the truth.'

Bl. Elizabeth of the Trinity

He alone loves the Creator perfectly who manifests a pure love for his neighbor.

St. Bede the Venerable

It is to those who have the most need of us that we ought to show our love more especially.

St. Francis de Sales

Everything comes from love, all is ordained for the salvation of man, God does nothing without this goal in mind.

St. Catherine of Siena

Charity unites us to God ... There is nothing mean in charity, nothing arrogant. Charity knows no schism, does not rebel, does all things in concord. In charity all the elect of God have been made perfect.

St. Clement I

Love is a fruit in season at all times, and within reach of every hand.

St. Teresa of Calcutta

The charity leading to the possession of God is not only charity, but solely the charity, the love that loved God above all things and loves God's creatures for God's sake.

St. Bonaventure

All our religion is but a false religion, and all our virtues are mere illusions and we ourselves are only hypocrites in the sight of God, if we have not that universal charity for everyone—for the good, and for the bad, for the poor and for the rich, and for all those who do us harm as much as those who do us good.

St. John Vianney

The things that we love tell us what we are.

St. Thomas Aquinas

PART FOUR

Prayer:

In Communication with God

Virtues are formed by prayer. Prayer preserves temperance. Prayer suppresses anger. Prayer prevents emotions of pride and envy. Prayer draws into the soul the Holy Spirit, and raises man to Heaven.

St. Ephraem of Syria

Why should we pray? Why breathe? We have to take in fresh air and get rid of bad air; we have to take in new power and get rid of old weaknesses. We pray because we are orchestras and always need to tune-up. Just as a battery sometimes runs down and needs to be charged, so we have to be renewed in spiritual vigor. Our blessed Lord said, 'Without Me you can do nothing.'

Ven. Fulton J. Sheen

The great method of prayer is to have none. If in going to prayer one can form in oneself a pure capacity for receiving the spirit of God, that will suffice for all methods.

St. Jane Frances de Chantal

The stillness of prayer is the most essential condition for fruitful action. Before all else, the disciple kneels down.

St. Gianna Beretta Molla

Hold prayer in high esteem. It is the foundation of all the virtues, and the source of all grace needed to sanctify ourselves and to discharge the duties of our employment.

St. Jean-Baptiste de la Salle

Pray with great confidence, with confidence based upon the goodness and generosity of God and upon the promises of Jesus Christ. God is a spring of living water which flows unceasingly into the hearts of those who pray.

St. Louis de Montfort

Action is worthless without prayer; prayer is worth more with sacrifice.

St. Josemaría Escrivá

Seek out with jealous care the place, time, and means most suited to quiet and contemplation, and lovingly embrace silence and solitude.

St. Albert the Great

Prayer is the raising of the mind to God.
We must always remember this. The actual words matter less.

St. John XXIII

Prayer is the best weapon we possess. It is the key that opens the heart of God.

St. Pio of Pietrelcina

For me prayer is a surge of the heart, it is a simple look towards Heaven, it is a cry of recognition and of love, embracing both trial and joy.

St.Thérèse of Lisieux

It is simply impossible to lead, without the aid of prayer, a virtuous life.

St. John Chrysostom

We must meditate before, during and after everything we do. The prophet says: 'I will pray, and then I will understand.' This is the way we can easily overcome the countless difficulties we have to face day after day, which, after all, are part of our work. In meditation we find the strength to bring Christ to birth in ourselves and in others.

St. Charles Borromeo

We must pray without ceasing, in every occurrence and employment of our lives, that prayer which is rather a habit of lifting up the heart to God as in a constant communication with Him.

St. Elizabeth Ann Seton

Arm yourself with prayer instead of a sword; wear humility instead of fine clothes.

St. Dominic

Real prayer is union with God, a union as vital as that of the vine to the branch.

St. Teresa of Calcutta

For continual prayer doth illumine, exalt, and transform the soul, and illumined by that light and uplifted by prayer, it doth clearly behold the way prepared for it and trodden already by the feet of the Crucified. Thus walking upon this way with an awakened heart, not only do we escape

from the heavy cares of this world, but we are
uplifted above ourselves and do taste of the
divine sweetness, and being thus uplifted we
are kindled with divine fire, and burning with
love, we are made one with God. And all this
cometh of gazing upon the Cross through
the medium of continual prayer.

Bl. Angela of Foligno

Prayer draws into the soul the Holy Spirit,
and raises man to Heaven.

St. Ephraem of Syria

With God, the prayers of the saints are the prayers of His friends, but the prayers of Mary are the prayers of His mother. Happy are they who confidently and at all times have recourse to this divine mother!

St. Alphonsus Maria de Liguori

Prayer is the remedy when temptations to sin rage in the heart. Whenever you are tempted to sin, pray, and pray earnestly. Frequent prayer renders powerless the assaults of vice.

St. Isidore of Seville

You should not think of prayer as being a matter of words. It is a desire for God, an indescribable devotion, not of human origin, but the gift of God's grace.

St. John Chrysostom

Read and re-read ceaselessly the Holy Gospel … so as to always have before one's mind the actions, words, and thoughts of Jesus, in order to think, speak and act like Jesus, to follow the examples and teachings of Jesus, not the examples and ways of behaving of the world. So easily do we fall into this latter, as soon as we take our eyes off the Divine Model.

Bl. Charles de Foucauld

How often I failed in my duty to God, because I was not leaning on the strong pillar of prayer.

St. Teresa of Avila

PART FIVE

Faith:

Trust in God's Providence

As to the past, let us entrust it to God's mercy, the future to divine providence. Our task is to live holy the present moment.

St. Gianna Beretta Molla

Remember that you have only one soul;
that you have only one death to die;
that you have only one life, which is short
and has to be lived by you alone; and there is
only one Glory, which is eternal. If you do
this, there will be many things about which
you care nothing.

St. Teresa of Avila

The more a person loves God, the more reason he has to hope in Him. This hope produces in the saints an unutterable peace, which they preserve even in adversity, because as they love God, and know how beautiful He is to those who love Him, they place all their confidence and find all their repose in Him alone.

St. Alphonsus di Liguori

To live without faith, without a heritage to defend, without battling constantly for truth, is not to live but to 'get along'. We must never just 'get along'.

Bl. Pier Giorgio Frassati

Take care of your body as if you were going to live forever. Take care of your soul as if you were going to die tomorrow.

St. Augustine

We shall steer safely through every storm so long as our heart is right, our intention fervent, our courage steadfast, and our trust fixed on God.

St. Francis de Sales

O life so dull and monotonous, how many treasures you contain! Through the eyes of faith, no two hours are alike, and the dullness and monotony disappear.

St. Faustina Kowalska

For man is by nature afraid of death and of the dissolution of the body; but there is this most startling fact, that he who has put on the faith of the Cross despises even what is naturally fearful, and for Christ's sake is not afraid of death.

St. Athanasius

It seems to me that if your confidence were as great as it ought to be, you would not worry about what may happen to you; you would place it all in God's hands, hoping that when He wants something of you He will let you know what it is.

St. Claude de la Colombière

It is not the actual physical exertion that counts towards one's progress, nor the nature of the task, but by the spirit of faith with which it is undertaken.

St. Francis Xavier

Always keep your faith in the love of God. If you have to suffer, it will be because you are deeply loved; so whatever happens, love and chant your thanksgiving.

Bl. Elizabeth of the Trinity

Sin is the cause of all this pain; but all shall be well, and all shall be well, and all manner of things shall be well.

St. Julian of Norwich

Faith seeks understanding that I may believe, but I believe in order to understand.

St. Anselm

Every moment comes to us pregnant with a command from God, only to pass on and plunge into eternity, there to remain forever what we have made of it.

St. Francis de Sales

To the Servant of God ... every place is the right place, every time the right time.

St. Catherine of Siena

Consult not your fears but your hopes and your dreams. Think not about your frustrations, but about your unfulfilled potential. Concern yourself not with what you tried and failed in, but with what it is still possible for you to do.

St. John XXIII

In all the events of life, you must recognize the Divine will. Adore and bless it, especially in the things which are the hardest for you.

St. Pio of Pietrelcina

Let us throw ourselves into His goodness, where every failing will be concealed and anxiety turned into love.

St. Paul of the Cross

PART SIX

Peace:

Creating a Dwelling Place
for the Lord

Keep your soul at peace, in order to be attentive and very faithful to the inner movement of the Holy Spirit.

St. Peter Julian Eymard

Never be in a hurry; do everything quietly and in a calm spirit. Do not lose your inner peace for anything whatsoever, even if your whole world seems upset.

St. Francis de Sales

A great means to preserve continual peace and tranquility of soul is to receive everything from the hands of God, both great and small, and in whatever way it comes.

St. Dorotheus of Gaza

See, my children, a person who is in a state of sin is always sad. Whatever he does, he is weary and disgusted with everything; while he who is at peace with God is always happy, always joyous … Oh, beautiful life! Oh, beautiful death!

St. Jean Marie Baptiste Vianney

We must sometimes bear with little defects in others, as we have, against our will, to bear with natural defects in ourselves. If we wish to keep peace with our neighbor, we should never remind anyone of his natural defects.

St. Philip Neri

Peace and union are the most necessary of all things for men who live in common, and nothing serves so well to establish and maintain them as the forbearing charity whereby we put up with another's defects. There is no one who has not his faults, and is not in some ways a burden to others, whether he be a superior or a subject, an old man or a young, a scholar or a dunce.

St. Robert Bellarmine

God's spirit is a spirit of peace, and even when we have serious faults, he grants us a tranquil, humbled, confident pain which depends entirely on His mercy.

St. Pio of Pietrelcina

Maintain a spirit of peace and you'll save a thousand souls.

St. Seraphim of Sarov

We must go out to Pure Life, Pure Truth, Pure Love, and that is the definition of God. He is the ultimate goal of life; from Him we came, and in Him alone do we find our peace.

Ven. Fulton J. Sheen

A peaceful man does more good than a learned one.

St. John XXIII

Thou hast made us for thyself and restless
is our heart until it comes to rest in thee.

St. Augustine

Who except God can give you peace?
Has the world ever been able to satisfy
the heart?

St. Gerard Majella

The fruit of silence is prayer. The fruit of prayer is faith. The fruit of faith is love. The fruit of love is service. The fruit of service is peace.

St. Teresa of Calcutta

Jesus is happy to come with us, as truth is happy to be spoken, as life to be lived, as light to be lit, as love is to be loved, as joy to be given, as peace to be spread.

St. Francis of Assisi

Keep close to the Catholic Church at all times, for the Church alone can give you true peace, since she alone possesses Jesus, the true Prince of Peace, in the Blessed Sacrament.

St. Pio of Pietrelcina

To be entirely conformed and resigned to the Divine Will, is truly a road in which we cannot get wrong, and is the only road which leads us to taste and enjoy that peace which sensual and earthly men know nothing of.

St. Philip Neri

There is no peace except in perfect forgetfulness of self; we must resolve to forget even our spiritual interests, so that we may seek nothing but God's glory.

St. Claude de la Colombière

Then shouldst thou readily and trustfully commit thyself and all that concerns thee to the unfailing and most sure Providence of God, in silence and peace. He Himself will fight for thee, and will grant thee a liberty and consolation better, nobler, and sweeter than would be possible if thou gavest thyself up day and night to thy fancies, to vain and wandering thoughts, which hold captive the mind … wearying soul and body, and wasting uselessly alike thy time and strength.

St. Albert the Great

Be at peace with your own soul; then Heaven and Earth will be at peace with you. Enter eagerly into the treasure house that is within you, and so you will see the things that are in Heaven; for there is one single door to them both.

St. Isaac the Syrian

The bee collects honey from flowers in such a way as to do the least damage or destruction to them, and he leaves them whole, undamaged and fresh, just as he found them.

St. Francis de Sales

PART SEVEN

Forgiveness:

Giving and Receiving Kindness

Forgiveness demonstrates the presence in the world of the love which is more powerful than sin.

St. John Paul II

No one heals himself by wounding another.

St. Ambrose

There are two ways of knowing how good and loving God is. One is by never losing Him, through the preservation of innocence, and the other is by finding Him after one has lost Him. Repentance is not self-regarding, but God-regarding. It is not self-loathing, but God-loving. Christianity bids us accept ourselves as we really are, with all our faults and our failings and our sins.

In all other religions, one has to be good to come to God—in Christianity one does not. Christianity might be described as a 'come as you are' party. It bids us stop worrying about ourselves, stop concentrating on our faults and our failings, and thrust them upon the Saviour with a firm resolve of amendment. The examination of conscience never induces despair, always hope …

Ven. Fulton J. Sheen

Prayer for our enemies is the very highest
summit of self-control.

St. John Chrysostom

Extend your mercy toward others, so that there can be no one in need whom you meet without helping. For what hope is there for us if God should withdraw His Mercy from us?

St. Vincent de Paul

The love of Christ knows no limits. It never ends; it does not shrink from ugliness and filth.

St. Teresa Benedicta of the Cross

We are not the sum of our weaknesses and failures; we are the sum of the Father's love for us and our real capacity to become the images of His Son.

St. John Paul II

Let no one mourn that he has fallen again and again; for forgiveness has risen from the grave.

St. John Chrysostom

There is still time for endurance, time for patience, time for healing, time for change. Have you slipped? Rise up. Have you sinned? Cease. Do not stand among sinners, but leap aside.

St. Basil

The way to overcome the devil when he excites feelings of hatred for those who injure is immediately to pray for their conversion.

St. John Vianney

Confession heals, confession justifies, confession grants pardon of sin. All hope consists in confession. In confession there is a chance for mercy. Believe it firmly. Do not doubt, do not hesitate, never despair of the mercy of God. Hope and have confidence in confession.

St. Isidore of Seville

For there are three ways of performing an act of mercy: the merciful word, by forgiving and by comforting; secondly, if you can offer no word, then pray that too is mercy; and thirdly, deeds of mercy. And when the Last Day comes, we shall be judged from this, and on this basis we shall receive the eternal verdict.

St. Faustina Kowalska

Fear and honor, praise and bless, thank and adore the Lord God Almighty, in Trinity and Unity, Father, Son, and Holy Spirit, Creator of all things. Do not put off any longer confessing all your sins, for death will soon come. Give and it will be given you; forgive and you will be forgiven ... Blessed are they who die repentant, for they shall go to the Kingdom of Heaven! But woe to those who are not converted, for these children of the Devil will go with their father into everlasting fire. Be watchful, therefore. Shun evil, and persevere in well-doing until the end.

St. Francis of Assisi

Forgiveness is the remission of sins. For it is by this that what has been lost, and was found, is saved from being lost again.

St. Augustine

While you are proclaiming peace with your lips, be careful to have it even more fully in your heart.

St. Francis of Assisi

There are many passages in Scripture where confession does not imply an expression of repentance so much as an expression of praise to God.

St. Jerome

Forgiveness is above all a personal choice,
a decision of the heart to go against the
natural instinct to pay back evil with evil.

St. John Paul II

There is no sin nor wrong that gives a man such a foretaste of hell in this life as anger and impatience.

St. Catherine of Siena

If a man finds it very hard to forgive injuries, let him look at a Crucifix, and think that Christ shed all His blood for him, and not only forgave His enemies, but even prayed His Heavenly Father to forgive them also.

St. Philip Neri

The ... thing that struck me was Our Lord's dispositions with regard to Judas who betrayed Him, to the apostles who abandoned Him, and to the priests and others who were the cause of the persecution He suffered. Amidst it all Jesus remained perfectly calm, His love for His disciples and enemies was not altered at all; He grieved over

the harm they did themselves, but His own
sufferings, far from troubling Him, comforted
Him because He knew they would act as a
remedy for the sins of His enemies. His Heart
was without bitterness and full of tenderness
toward His enemies in spite of their perfidy
and of all they made Him suffer.

St. Claude de la Colombière

Let all bitterness, and anger, and indignation, and clamour, and blasphemy, be put away from you, with all malice. And be … kind to one another; merciful, forgiving one another, even as God hath forgiven you in Christ.

St. Paul the Apostle

God will not deny His mercy to anyone. Heaven and Earth may change, but God's mercy will never be exhausted.

St. Faustina Kowalska

How about the sin, then, of a husband and wife, of a brother and sister, who spew out all sorts of blasphemies upon one another? They would tear out one another's eyes if they could, or even take away each other's lives … They do not appreciate what they are saying. Alas! Unhappy people, your curses take effect more often than you think … But what should we do then? This is what we should do. We should make use of all the annoyances that happen to us to remind ourselves that since we are in revolt against God, it is but just that other creatures should revolt against us. We should never give others occasion to curse us … If something irritating or troublesome happens, instead of loading with curses whatever is not going the way we want it, it would be just as easy and a great deal more beneficial for us to say: 'God bless it!'

St. Jean Marie Baptiste Vianney

To harbor no envy, no anger, no resentment against an offender is still not to have charity for him. It is possible, without any charity, to avoid rendering evil for evil. But to render, spontaneously, good for evil—such belongs to a perfect spiritual love.

St. Maximus the Confessor

He who knows how to forgive prepares for himself many graces from God. As often as I look upon the cross, so often will I forgive with all my heart.

St. Faustina

PART EIGHT

Suffering:
Offering Up our Troubles

All the science of the saints is included in these two things: To do, and to suffer. And whoever had done these two things best, has made himself most saintly.

St. Francis de Sales

Love and suffering are clearly linked,
like the sun and the light. We cannot
love without suffering and we cannot suffer
without love.

St. Gianna Beretta Molla

I cannot ... inflict great sufferings upon myself,
but I can sacrifice my will each minute.

Bl. Elizabeth of the Trinity

All life demands struggle. Those who have everything given to them become lazy, selfish, and insensitive to the real values of life. The very striving and hard work that we so constantly try to avoid is the major building block in the person we are today.

Bl. Paul VI

If there be a true way that leads to the Everlasting Kingdom, it is most certainly that of suffering, patiently endured.

St. Colette

Trials are nothing else but the forge that purifies the soul of all its imperfections.

St. Mary Magdalen De'Pazzi

I could not always live at ease. Of what means, then, would He make use?

St. Thérèse of Lisieux

God never tries us beyond what we are able to suffer. Oh, I fear nothing; if God sends such great suffering to a soul. He upholds it with an even greater grace, although we are not aware of it.

St. Faustina Kowalska

The souls that are the most dear to My Father are those He tries the most, and the greatness of their trials is the measure of His Love.

St. Thérèse of Lisieux

Whenever we are oppressed by various anxieties ... let us confer that it is only right for us to endure it, that the Scripture may be fulfilled in us.

St. Jerome

Suffering, if it is accepted together, if it is borne together, is joy.

St. Teresa of Calcutta

I realized that if all went well I would not have had that opportunity to love Jesus. And I'm so happy.

Bl. Chiara Badano

Spiritual persons ought to be equally ready to experience sweetness and consolation in the things of God, or to suffer and keep their ground in dryness of spirit and devotion, and for as long as God pleases, without their making any complaint about it.

St. Philip Neri

If God sends you many sufferings, it is a sign that He has great plans for you and certainly wants to make you a saint.

St. Ignatius of Loyola

We rejoice in our sufferings because we know that suffering produces perseverance; perseverance, character; and character, hope. And hope does not disappoint us, because God has poured out his love into our hearts by the Holy Spirit, who He has given us.

St. Paul the Apostle

I should not dare to detach my gaze, well knowing that beyond the dark clouds the sweet Sun still shines.

St. Thérèse of Lisieux

Tribulation ... a gracious gift of God, a gift that He specially gave His special friends.

St. Thomas More

The more we are afflicted in this world, the greater is our assurance in the next; the more sorrow in the present, the greater will be our joy in the future.

St. Isidore of Seville

If you suffer with Him, with Him you will reign, grieving with Him, with Him you will rejoice, dying with Him on the cross of tribulation, with Him you will possess mansions in Heaven among the splendors of the saints.

St. Clare of Assisi

Mental and physical suffering is everywhere. Pain and suffering have to come into your life but remember pain, sorrow, suffering are but the kiss of Jesus—signs that you have come so close to Him that He can kiss you. Accept them as a gift—all for Jesus.

St. Teresa of Calcutta

There is no more evident sign that anyone is a saint and of the number of the elect, than to see him leading a good life and at the same time a prey to desolation, suffering, and trials.

St. Aloysius Gonzaga

He who can preserve gentleness amid pains, and peace amid worry about a multitude of affairs, is almost perfect.

St. Francis de Sales

This, in short, is the difference between us and others who know not God, that in misfortune they complain and murmur, while the adversity does not call us away from the truth of virtue and faith, but strengthens us by its suffering.

St. Cyprian

When you encounter difficulties and
contradictions, do not try to break
them, but bend them with gentleness and time.

St. Francis de Sales

If the Lord should give you power to raise the dead, He would give much less than He does when He bestows suffering. By miracles you would make yourself debtor to Him, while by suffering He may become debtor to you. And even if sufferings had no other reward than being able to bear something for that God who loves you, is not this a great reward and a sufficient remuneration? Whoever loves, understands what I say.

St. John Chrysostom

The more we are afflicted in this world, the greater is our assurance in the next; the more sorrow in the present, the greater will be our joy in the future.

St. Isadore of Seville

PART NINE

Joy:
Experiencing Eternity in Time

Joy is not the same as pleasure or happiness. A wicked and evil man may have pleasure, while any ordinary mortal is capable of being happy. Pleasure generally comes from things, and always through the senses; happiness comes from humans through fellowship. Joy comes from loving God and neighbor. Pleasure is quick and violent, like a flash of lightning. Joy is steady and abiding, like a fixed star. Pleasure depends on external circumstances, such as money, food, travel, etc. Joy is independent of them, for it comes from a good conscience and love of God.

Ven. Fulton J. Sheen

Joy is a net of love by which we catch souls.

St. Teresa of Calcutta

Be merry, really merry. The life of a true Christian should be perpetual jubilee, a prelude to the festivals of eternity.

St. Theophane Venard

We are not saints yet, but we, too, should beware. Uprightness and virtue do have their rewards, in self-respect and in respect from others, and it is easy to find ourselves aiming for the result rather than the cause. Let us aim for joy, rather than respectability. Let us make fools of ourselves from time to time, and thus see ourselves, for a moment, as the all-wise God sees us.

St. Philip Neri

Joy, with peace, is the sister of charity. Serve the Lord with laughter.

St. Pio of Pietrelcina

The secret of happiness is to live moment by moment and to thank God for all that He, in his goodness, sends to us day after day.

St. Gianna Beretta Molla

Christian joy is a gift of God flowing from a good conscience.

St. Philip Neri

Since happiness is nothing other than the enjoyment of the highest good and since the highest good is above, no one can be happy unless he rises above himself, not by an ascent of the body, but of the heart.

St. Bonaventure

It is requisite for the relaxation of the mind that we make use, from time to time, of playful deeds and jokes.

St. Thomas Aquinas

Two classes of people make up the world: those who have found God, and those who are looking for Him, thirsting, hungering, seeking! And the great sinners came closer to Him than the proud intellectuals! Pride swells and inflates the ego; gross sinners are depressed, deflated and empty. They, therefore, have room for God. God prefers a loving sinner to a loveless 'saint'. Love can be trained; pride cannot. The man who thinks that he knows will rarely find truth; the man who knows he is a miserable, unhappy sinner, like the woman at the well, is closer to peace, joy and salvation than he knows.

Ven. Fulton J. Sheen

The end for which we are created invites us to walk a road that is surely sown with a lot of thorns, but it is not sad; through even the sorrow, it is illuminated by joy.

Bl. Pier Giorgio Frassati

Happy is the youth, because he has time before him to do good.

St. Philip Neri

O joy that flows from the knowledge of one's self! O unchanging Truth. Your constancy is everlasting!

St. Faustina Kowalska

I know no greater joy than to discover some weaknesses in myself that I did not realize before. I often taste this joy and shall always have it when God gives me his light when I am examining my conscience.

St. Claude de la Colombière

A heart filled with joy is more easily made perfect than one that is sad.

St. Philip Neri

Spiritual joy arises from purity of the heart
and perseverance in prayer.

St. Francis of Assisi

Ponder in mind on the joy of Heaven, talk it over with yourself, love it with all your heart and speak of it to others. Let your soul hunger and your body thirst for it. Long for it with all your being until at last you enter into the joy of your Lord!

St. Anselm

What measure men put to their love of God here will be the measure of their rejoicing of God in Heaven. Therefore, love God intensely here and your rejoicing will be intense hereafter. Continue to grow in the love of God here, and afterwards in Heaven you will possess the fullness of eternal joy.

St. Bonaventure

PART TEN

Grace:
God's Transformational Gift

For by grace you are saved through faith, and that not of yourselves; for it is the gift of God; Not of works, that no man may glory.

St. Paul the Apostle

He who aspires to the grace of God must be pure, with a heart as innocent as a child's. Purity of a heart is to God like a perfume, sweet and agreeable.

St. Nicholas of Flüe

Christian optimism is not a sugary optimism, nor is it a mere human confidence that everything will turn out alright. It is an optimism that sinks its roots into an awareness of our freedom, and the sure knowledge of the power of grace. It is an optimism that leads us to make demands on ourselves, to struggle to respond at every moment to God's call.

St. Josemaría Escrivá

God is touched by our sorrows and does not allow them to last for ever. He takes pleasure in trying our love for a time because he sees that trials purify us and render us worthy to receive his greater graces.

St. Claude de la Colombière

Let us not forget this truth: the moment a man, by the help of God, succeeds in overcoming his own will, that is, in freeing himself from every inordinate affection and care, to cast himself and all his miseries unreservedly into the bosom of God, that moment he becomes so pleasing to God that he receives the gift of grace. Grace brings charity, and charity drives out all fear and hesitation, and fills the soul with confidence and hope.

St. Albert the Great

Grace is nothing else but a certain
beginning of glory in us.

St. Thomas Aquinas

There is no saint without a past, no sinner without a future.

St. Augustine

Grace does not work like a penny in the slot machine. Grace will move you only when you want it to move you, and only when you let it move you. The supernatural order supposes the freedom of the natural order, but does not destroy it.

Ven. Fulton J. Sheen

We know certainly that our God calls us to a holy life. We know that He gives us every grace, every abundant grace; and though we are so weak of ourselves, this grace is able to carry us through every obstacle and difficulty.

St. Elizabeth Ann Seton

No one can become blessed, unless he ascends above his very self ... but we are not able to be raised above ourselves unless by means of a superior virtue raising us. For however much as interior steps are arranged, nothing is done, unless the Divine Assistance accompanies.

St. Bonaventure

If any of you lacks wisdom, let him ask God, who gives to all men generously and without reproaching, and it will be given him.

St. James the Apostle

Devotion to the Blessed Virgin is actually necessary, because there is no better means of obtaining God's graces than through His most holy mother.

St. Philip Neri

Understand this well: there is something holy, something divine hidden in the most ordinary situations, and it is up to each one of you to discover.

St. Josemaría Escrivá

I have promised with God's grace not to begin any action without remembering that He is witness of it—that He performs it together with me and gives me the means to do it.

St. Claude de la Colombière

To change that which is dust into light, to make pure that which is unclean, holy that which is sinful, to make the creature like its Creator, man like God ... only God by His grace, by His abundant extraordinary grace, can accomplish it.

St. Louis de Montfort

Few souls understand what God would accomplish in them if they were to abandon themselves unreservedly to Him and if they were to allow His grace to mold them accordingly.

St. Ignatius of Loyola

Things were in God's plan which I had not planned at all. I am coming to the living faith and conviction that—from God's point of view—there is no chance and that the whole of my life, down to every detail, has been mapped out in God's divine providence and makes complete and perfect sense in God's all-seeing eyes.

St. Teresa Benedicta of the Cross

It all comes to this, then: that you should find an easy means for obtaining from God the grace necessary to make you holy ... Now, I say that to find this grace of God, we must find Mary.

St. Louis de Montfort

Without the burden of afflictions it is impossible to reach the height of grace. The gift of grace increases as the struggle increases.

St. Rose of Lima

Few souls understand what God would accomplish in them if they were to abandon themselves unreservedly to Him and if they were to allow His grace to mold them accordingly.

St. Ignatius Loyola

PART ELEVEN

Work:

Embracing Responsibility with Joy

If we are doing any type of good work, we should season our actions with the desire and remembrance of God.

St. John Chrysostom

One earns Paradise with one's daily task.

St. Gianna Beretta Molla

Learn to do thy part and leave the rest to Heaven.

Bl. John Henry Newman

The first end I propose in our daily work is to do the will of God; secondly, to do it in the manner He wills it; and thirdly to do it because it is His will.

St. Elizabeth Ann Seton

The approach to perfect prayer is when a man is freed from dispersion of thoughts and sees his mind, enlightened in the Lord, filled with joy. A man has attained perfection in prayer if he makes himself dead to the world with its ease. But when a man does his work diligently for the sake of God, it is not a distraction but a thoroughness, which pleases God.

St. Barsanuphius

A servant is not good if she is not industrious; work-shy piety in people of our position is sham piety. All devotion which leads to sloth is false. We must love work.

St. Zita

Turn your back on the tempter when he whispers in your ear: 'Why make life difficult for yourself?'

St. Josemaría Escrivá

Actions speak louder than words; let your words teach and your actions speak.

St. Anthony of Padua

Let go of your plans. The first hour of your morning belongs to God. Tackle the day's work that He charges you with, and He will give you the power to accomplish it.

St. Teresa Benedicta of the Cross

Often in my desire to work for others I find my hands tied, something hinders my charitable designs, some hostile influence renders me powerless. My prayers seem to avail nothing, my kind acts are rejected, I seem to do wrong things when I am trying to do my best. In such cases I must not grieve. I am only treading in my Master's steps.

St. Katherine Drexel

This labor of ours is brief, but the reward is eternal; let the noises of the fleeting world and its shadow not confound you.

St. Clare of Assisi

All creation praises God not in word but in deed.

St. Jerome

Remember that the Christian life is one of action; not of speech and daydreams. Let there be few words and many deeds, and let them be done well.

St. Vincent Pallotti

We are at Jesus' disposal. If He wants you to be sick in bed, if He wants you to proclaim His work in the street, if He wants you to clean the toilets all day, that's all right, everything is all right. We must say, 'I belong to you. You can do whatever you like.' And this is our strength. This is the joy of the Lord.

St. Teresa of Calcutta

Pray and be always vigilant. And the work that you began ... finish, and the ministry you assumed ... fulfill, in holy poverty and sincere humility.

St. Clare of Assisi

'Great' holiness consists in carrying out
the 'little duties' of each moment.

St. Josemarìa Escrivá

I would remind you that many forget what they hear. They are not numbered among the wise. The truly wise man acts, and does zealously what the Law prescribes.

St. Bonaventure

Pray as though everything depended on God. Work as though everything depended on you.

St. Augustine

There are different kinds of gifts, but the same Spirit. There are different kinds of service, but the Lord. There are different kinds of working, but the same God works all of them in men.

St. Paul the Apostle

Put your heart aside. Duty comes first. But when fulfilling your duty, put your heart into it. It helps.

St. Josemaría Escrivá

We ourselves feel that what we are doing is just a drop in the ocean. But if the drop was not in the ocean, I think the ocean would be less because of the missing drop.

St. Teresa of Calcutta

Jacob did not cease to be a saint because he had to attend to his flocks.

St. Teresa of Avila

PART TWELVE

Divine Intimacy:

In Communication with God

As all men are touched by God's love, so all are also touched by the desire for His intimacy. No one escapes this longing; we are all kings in exile, miserable without the Infinite. Those who reject the grace of God have a desire to avoid God, as those who accept it have a desire for God.

Ven. Fulton J. Sheen

Only one thing is impossible for man—
to avoid death. To have communion with
God is possible for him, if he understands
how it is possible. For if he wishes and
understands [how it is to be done] through
faith and love, testified by a good life, a man
can commune with God.

St. Anthony of Egypt

To love God with your whole heart it is requisite that nothing attract your heart more than God attracts it. You must not take more pleasure in the things of Earth than in God. Honors and places of position, love of father and mother and relatives must not count in the scale of love before love of God. Be it friend or relative, place or position, be it what it may, if anything takes up your heart's love more than God, you do not love God with your whole heart.

St. John Chrysostom

They deceive themselves who believe that union with God consists in ecstasies or raptures, and in the enjoyment of Him. For it consists in nothing except the surrender and subjection of our will with our thoughts, words and actions to the will of God.

St. Teresa of Avila

It is of the greatest importance for the soul to exercise itself much in love, so that attaining rapidly to perfection it may not be detained here below, but may soon see God face to face.

St. John of the Cross

Consider all the past as nothing, and say,
like David: Now I begin to love my God.

St. Francis de Sales

The true friend of Jesus Christ must be so united by his intelligence and will to the Divine will and goodness that his imagination and passions have no hold over him, and that he troubles not whether men give him love or ridicule, nor heeds what may be done to him. Know well that a truly good will does all and is of more value than all.

St. Albert the Great

Grant me, O Lord my God, a mind to know you, a heart to seek you, wisdom to find you, conduct pleasing to you, faithful perseverance in waiting for you, and a hope of finally embracing you.

St. Thomas Aquinas

He did not barely create man, as He did all the irrational creatures on Earth, but made them after His own image, giving them a portion even of the power of His own Word; so that having as it were a kind of reflection of the Word, and being made rational, they might be able to abide ever in blessedness, living the true life which belongs to the saints in paradise.

St. Athanasius

What is man created for? In order that, through the knowledge of God's creatures, he should see God Himself and should glorify Him, Who has created them for man. A mind cleaving to God by love (a God-loving and God-beloved mind) is an invisible blessing, given by God to the worthy for their good life.

St. Anthony of Egypt

It is written: 'When thou shalt pray, enter into thy chamber'—i.e., into the inmost abode of thy heart—and, 'having shut the door' of thy senses, with a pure heart, a free conscience and an unfeigned faith, 'pray to thy Father' in spirit and in truth, in the 'secret' of thy soul. Then only will a man attain this ideal, when he has despoiled and

stripped himself of all else; when, wholly
recollected within himself, he has hidden
from and forgotten the whole world, that he
may abide in silence in the presence of Jesus
Christ ... With all the intensity of his love he
pours forth his heart before Him, in sincerity
and truth, until he loses himself in God.

St. Albert the Great

Place your mind in the mirror of eternity;
Place your soul in the splendor of glory;
Place your heart in the figure of the divine
substance; And through contemplation,
transform your entire being into the image
of the Divine One Himself, so that you,
yourself, may also experience what His
friends experience when they taste the hidden
sweetness that God alone has kept from the
beginning for those who love Him.

St. Clare of Assisi

He who wishes for anything but Christ, does not know what he wishes; he who asks for anything but Christ, does not know what he is asking; he who works, and not for Christ, does not know what he is doing.

St. Philip Neri

In the first creation He gave me myself; but in His new creation He gave me Himself, and by that gift restored to me the self that I had lost.

St. Bernard of Clairvaux

When shall it be that we shall taste the sweetness of the Divine Will in all that happens to us, considering in everything only His good pleasure, by whom it is certain that adversity is sent with as much love as prosperity, and as much for our good? When shall we cast ourselves undeservedly into the arms of our most loving Father in Heaven, leaving to Him the care of ourselves and of our affairs, and reserving only the desire of pleasing Him, and of serving Him well in all that we can?

St. Jane Frances de Chantal

To love God as He ought to be loved, we must be detached from all temporal love. We must love nothing but Him, or if we love anything else, we must love it only for His sake.

St. Peter Claver

We need no wings to go in search of Him, but have only to look upon Him present within us.

St. Teresa of Avila

The last thing I ask of you—and I ask it in the name of our Lord Jesus Christ—is that you love Him alone, that you trust implicitly in Him and that you encourage one another continually to suffer for the love of Him.

St. Mary Magdalen De'Pazzi

You pay God a compliment by asking great things of Him.

St. Teresa of Avila

PART THIRTEEN

Prudence:

Discerning God's Will

No one can come to Jesus unless he
is carried by these four virtues ...
prudence, fortitude, temperance, and justice.

St. Anthony of Padua

Prudence is the knowledge of what to seek and what to avoid.

St. Augustine

In matters of prudence, man stands in
very great need of being taught by others,
especially by old folk who have acquired a sane
understanding of the ends in practical matters.

St. Thomas Aquinas

A prudent man is one who sees as it were from afar, for his sight is keen, and he foresees the event of uncertainties.

St. Isidore of Seville

Let us employ the gift of reason for actions of prudence. Let us learn now abstinence from what is wicked, that we may not be forced to learn in the future. Let us employ life as a training school for what is good; and let us be roused to the hatred of sin. Let us bear about a deep love for the Creator; let us cleave to Him with our whole heart; let us not wickedly waste the substance of reason, like the prodigal. Let us obtain the joy laid up, in which Paul exulting, exclaimed, 'Who shall separate us from the love of Christ?' (Rom. 8.35). To Him belongs glory and honor, with the Father and the Holy Spirit, world without end. Amen.

St Clement of Alexandria

Blessed the one who does not speak through hope of reward, who is not always ready to unburden himself of his secrets, who is not anxious to speak, but who reflects prudently on what he is to say and the manner in which he is to reply.

St. Francis of Assisi

Wisdom is in the savoring of contemplation; Prudence is in foreseeing dangers; Strength is in bearing adversities; Understanding is in rejecting evil and choosing good ... He [The Lord] is prudence ... Learn this wisdom, O man, that you may be wise; this prudence, that you may take care of yourself.

St. Anthony of Padua

It would be the greatest delight of the seraphs to pile up sand on the seashore or to pull weeds in a garden for all eternity, if they found out such was God's will. Our Lord Himself teaches us to ask to do the will of God on Earth as the saints do it in Heaven: 'Thy will be done on Earth as it is in Heaven.'

St. Alphonsus Maria de Liguori

Understanding is the reward of faith. Therefore, seek not to understand that thou mayest believe, but believe that thou mayest understand.

St. Augustine

That we may not be deceived by self-love, in considering matters that concern us, we ought to look at them as if they belonged to others, and our only business with them was to give our judgement—not from interest, but in the cause of truth; and in the same way we should look on others' affairs as our own.

St. Ignatius Loyola

On each occasion, I say: 'Lord, thy will be done! It's not what this or that one wants, but what You want me to do.' This my fortress, this is my firm rock, this is my sure support.

St. John Chrysostom

Thus understanding and love, that is, the knowledge of and delight in the truth, are, as it were, the two arms of the soul, with which it embraces and comprehends with all the saints the length and breadth, the height and depth, that is the eternity, the love, the goodness, and the wisdom of God.

St. Bernard

Whatever did not fit in with my plan did lie within the plan of God. I have an ever deeper and firmer belief that nothing is merely an accident when seen in the light of God, that my whole life down to the smallest details has been marked out for me in the plan of Divine Providence and has a completely coherent meaning in God's all-seeing eyes. And so I am beginning to rejoice in the light of glory wherein this meaning will be unveiled to me.

St. Teresa Benedicta of the Cross

Above all, do not be your own master,
relying on your own prudence, contrary
to the caution of the wise man.

St. Ignatius

We judge all things according to the divine truth.

St. Augustine

He who follows his own ideas in opposition to the direction of his superiors needs no devil to tempt him, for he is a devil to himself.

St. John Climacus

All that is done by obedience is meritorious ... It is obedience, which, by the light of Faith, puts self-will to death, and causes the obedient man to despise his own will and throw himself into the arms of his superior ... Placed in the bark of obedience, he passes happily through the stormy sea of this life, in peace of soul and tranquility of heart. Obedience and faith disperse darkness; he is strong because he has no longer any weakness or fears, for self-will, which is the cause of inordinate fear and weakness, has been destroyed.

St. Catherine of Siena

PART FOURTEEN

Fortitude:

Sustenance for the Journey

What shall I say of fortitude, without which neither wisdom nor justice is of any worth? Fortitude is not of the body, but is a constancy of soul; wherewith we are conquerors in righteousness, patiently bear all adversities, and in prosperity are not puffed up. This fortitude he lacks who is overcome by pride, anger, greed, drunkenness, and the like. Neither have they fortitude who when in adversity make shift to escape at their souls' expense; wherefore the Lord saith, 'Fear not those who kill the body, but cannot kill the soul.' In like manner, those who are puffed up in prosperity and abandon themselves to excessive joviality cannot be called strong. For how can they be called strong who cannot hide and repress the heart's emotion? Fortitude is never conquered, or if conquered, is not fortitude.

St. Bruno

The person with fortitude is one who perseveres in doing what his conscience tells him he ought to do. He does not measure the value of a task exclusively by the benefit he receives from it, but rather by the service he renders to others. The strong man will at times suffer, but he stands firm; he may be driven to tears, but he will brush them aside. When difficulties come thick and fast, he does

not bend before them. Remember the example
given us in the book of the Machabees: an old
man, Eleazar, prefers to die rather than break
God's law. 'By manfully giving up my life now,
I will show myself worthy of my old age and
leave to the young a noble example of how to
die a good death willingly and nobly for the
revered and holy laws.'

St. Josemaria Escriva

Fortitude is the disposition of soul which enables us to despise all inconveniences and the loss of things not in our power.

St. Augustine

Remember that you will derive strength by reflecting that the saints yearn for you to join their ranks; desire to see you fight bravely, and behave like a true knight in your encounters with the same adversities which they had to conquer, and that breath-taking joy is their eternal reward for having endured a few years of temporal pain. Every drop of earthly bitterness will be changed into an ocean of heavenly sweetness.

Bl. Henry Suso

When one is convinced that his cause is just, he will fear nothing.

St. John Bosco

In so far as divine love beautifies our souls, and makes us pleasing to His divine Majesty, it is called grace; in so far as it gives us strength to do good, it is called charity; but when it reaches such a degree of perfection, that it makes us not only do good, but do so carefully, frequently and readily, then it is called devotion.

St. Francis de Sales

Consider seriously how quickly people change, and how little trust is to be had in them; and hold fast to God, Who does not change.

St. Teresa of Avila

It is better to say one 'Our Father' fervently and devoutly than a thousand with no devotion and full of distraction.

St. Edmund

I do not fear at all what men can do to me for speaking the truth. I only fear what God would do if I were to lie.

St. John Bosco

Great are those two gifts, wisdom and continence: wisdom, forsooth, whereby we are formed in the knowledge of God; continence whereby we are not conformed to this world.

St. Augustine

The principal act of courage is to endure and withstand dangers doggedly rather than to attack them.

St. Thomas Aquinas

I never shrink from any undertaking which I know is good and necessary, no matter what the difficulties. If, for example, I must see some unfriendly important person, I don't hesitate, but first I recite a Hail Mary. I do the same before calling on anybody. Then, come what may, I do my best and leave the rest to the Lord.

St. John Bosco

Though the path is plain and smooth for men of good will, he who walks it will not travel far, and will do so only with difficulty, if he does not have good feet: that is, courage and a persevering spirit.

St. John of the Cross

To have courage for whatever comes in life,
everything lies in that.

St. Teresa of Avila

As soon as worldly people see that you wish to follow a devout life, they aim a thousand darts of mockery and even detraction at you. The most malicious of them will slander your conversion as hypocrisy, bigotry, and trickery. They will say that the world has turned against you and being rebuffed by it you have turned to God. Your friends will raise a host of objections which

they consider very prudent and charitable.
They will tell you that you will become
depressed, lose your reputation in the world,
be unbearable, and grow old before your time,
and that your affairs at home will suffer.
You must live in the world like one in the
world. They will say that you can save your
soul without going to such extremes, and a
thousand similar trivialities.

St. Francis de Sales

We must often draw the comparison between time and eternity. This is the remedy of all our troubles. How small will the present moment appear when we enter that great ocean.

St. Elizabeth Ann Seton

Your first task is to be dissatisfied with yourself, fight sin, and transform yourself into something better. Your second task is to put up with the trials and temptations of this world that will be brought on by the change in your life and to persevere to the very end in the midst of these things.

St. Augustine

Do not grieve over the temptations you suffer. When the Lord intends to bestow a particular virtue on us, He often permits us first to be tempted by the opposite vice. Therefore, look upon every temptation as an invitation to grow in a particular virtue and a promise by God that you will be successful, if only you stand fast.

St. Philip Neri

After knowing the will of God in regard to a work which we undertake, we should continue courageously, however difficult it may be. We should follow it to the end with as much constancy as the obstacles we encounter are great.

St. Vincent de Paul

Whoever from deep within her noble and zealous heart wishes to take up the cross, let her first take up the arms necessary for such battles; first is diligence; second, distrust of self; third, confidence in God; fourth, memory of his Passion; fifth, memory of one's own death; sixth, memory of the glory of God; seventh and last, the authority of Holy Scripture following the example of Christ Jesus in the desert.

St. Catherine of Bologna

Do not look forward to what may happen tomorrow; the same everlasting Father who cares for you today will take care of you tomorrow and every day. Either He will shield you from suffering, or He will give you unfailing strength to bear it.

St. Francis de Sales

It is good to think about our having our citizenship in Heaven and the saints of Heaven as our fellow citizens ... Then it is easier to bear the things that are on Earth.

St. Edith Stein

We must love Christ and always seek
Christ's embraces. Then everything
difficult will seem easy.

St. Jerome

Do not let any occasion of gaining merit pass without taking care to draw some spiritual profit from it; as, for example, from a sharp word which someone may say to you; from an act of obedience imposed against your will; from an opportunity which may occur to humble yourself, or to practice charity, sweetness, and patience. All of these occasions are gain for you, and you should seek to procure them; and at the close of that day, when the greatest number of them have come to you, you should go to rest most cheerful and pleased …

St. Ignatius Loyola

Though perseverance does not come from our power, yet it comes from within our power.

St. Francis de Sales

PART FIFTEEN

Gratitude:

Living Life with Grace

In all created things discern the providence
and wisdom of God, and in all things give
Him thanks.

St. Teresa of Avila

L et us thank God for His priceless gift!

St. Paul

No duty is more urgent than that of returning thanks.

St. Ambrose

A man wanted to do evil, but first prayed as usual; and finding himself prevented by God, he was then extremely thankful.

St. Mark the Ascetic

Out of gratitude and love for Him, we should desire to be reckoned fools.

St. Ignatius of Loyola

O my God, let me remember with gratitude and confess to Thee Thy mercies toward me.

St. Augustine of Hippo

O God, grant that whatever good things I have, I may share generously with those who have not, and whatever good things I do not have, I may request humbly from those who do.

St. Thomas Aquinas

Lord, teach me to be generous. Teach me to serve You as You deserve.

St. Ignatius of Loyola

In everything give thanks: for this is the will of God.

St. Paul

Does not the gratitude of the dog put to shame any man who is ungrateful to his benefactors?

St. Basil

B loom where you are planted.

St. Francis de Sales

Happiness can only be achieved by looking inward and learning to enjoy whatever life has and this requires transforming greed into gratitude.

St. John Chrysostom

Teach us to give and not count the cost.

St. Ignatius de Loyola

The best way to show my gratitude to God is to accept everything, even my problems, with joy.

St. Teresa of Calcutta

About the Compilers

Andrea Kirk Assaf has had the rare privilege of covering three pontificates in the span of a decade—the pontificates of John Paul II, Benedict XVI, and Francis. Andrea has written for *Inside the Vatican* magazine and several other Catholic and secular news outlets, covering World Youth Day in Toronto, the funeral of John Paul II, the election of Pope Benedict XVI, and now the popularity of the first successor of St. Peter from the New World, Pope Francis. Along with her husband Tony Assaf, an editor-journalist-translator, and their three children, Andrea divides her days between the Eternal City of Rome and a rural homestead in Remus, Michigan.

Kelly Anne Leahy graduated in 2014 with a BA in humanities from Villanova University, where she first encountered the powerful writings of the saints. Following graduation, she volunteered as a teacher for Mother Teresa's Missionaries of Charity in India. In 2015, Kelly was named a Wilbur Fellow at the Russell Kirk Center for Cultural Renewal in Mecosta, Michigan, where she began working with co-editor Andrea Kirk Assaf to develop a Catholic homeschooling model. Kelly currently lives in Rome, where she continues to learn about the unique role the saints play in Catholic spirituality.

Reader's Journal